Poison Petals
Don't Eat!

by Ellen Lawrence

Consultants:

Suzy Gazlay, MA
Recipient, Presidential Award for Excellence in Science Teaching

Dr. Robin Wall Kimmerer
Professor of Environmental and Forest Biology
SUNY College of Environmental Science and Forestry, Syracuse, New York

Kimberly Brenneman, PhD
National Institute for Early Education Research, Rutgers University
New Brunswick, New Jersey

BEARPORT
PUBLISHING

New York, New York

Credits

Cover © ArturKo/Shutterstock and © Nancy Kennedy/Shutterstock and © Gert Johannes Jacobus Very; 3L, © Richard Griffin/Shutterstock; 3TR, © Melinda Fawver/Shutterstock; 3BR, © picturepartners/Shutterstock; 4–5, © Richard Griffin/Shutterstock and © ppart/Shutterstock; 5, © Nancy Kennedy/Shutterstock and © Gert Johannes Jacobus Very; 6, © Le Do/Shutterstock and © Michael Peuckert/Imagebroker/FLPA; 7, © Karoline Cullen/Shutterstock; 8B, © Maxim Kulko/Shutterstock; 9, © Michael Dietrich/Imagebroker/Alamy; 9BR, © RF Company/Alamy; 10, © joingate/Shutterstock; 11T, © Nancy Kennedy/Shutterstock; 11BL, © Richard Griffin/Shutterstock; 11BR, © Bambuh/Shutterstock; 12, © Derek Middleton/FLPA; 13L, © Nino Barbieri/Wikipedia Creative Commons; 13C, © U.S. Fish and Wildlife Service; 13R, © Martin Fowler/Shutterstock; 14, © LianeM/Shutterstock; 15, © S & D & K Maslowski/FLPA; 16, © blickwinkel/Koenig/Alamy; 17, © James Schwabel/Alamy; 17B, © Steve Hurst/USDA; 18, © Cosmographics; 19L, © Jean E. Roche/Naturepl; 19LB, © Hans Hillewaert/Wikipedia Creative Commons; 20L, © Melinda Fawver/Shutterstock; 20R, © Jeff Banke/Shutterstock; 21, © Monkey Business Images/Shutterstock; 21B, © Chris Hill/Shutterstock; 22, © aopsan/Shutterstock; 23TL, © Cosmographics; 23TC, © Martin Fowler/Shutterstock; 23TR, © joingate/Shutterstock; 23BL, © a40757/Shutterstock; 23BC, © carroteater/Shutterstock; 23BR, © Nigel Cattlin/FLPA.

Publisher: Kenn Goin
Editorial Director: Adam Siegel
Creative Director: Spencer Brinker
Design: Elaine Wilkinson
Photo Researcher: Ruby Tuesday Books Ltd

Library of Congress Cataloging-in-Publication Data

Lawrence, Ellen, 1967–
  Poison petals : don't eat! / by Ellen Lawrence.
    p. cm. — (Plant-ology)
  Includes bibliographical references and index.
  ISBN 978-1-61772-590-6 (library binding) — ISBN 1-61772-590-0 (library binding)
  1. Poisonous plants—Juvenile literature. I. Title.
  QK100.A1L39 2013
  581.6'59—dc23
                            2012018639

For more information, write to Bearport Publishing Company, Inc., 45 West 21st Street, Suite 3B, New York, New York 10010. Printed in the United States of America.

10 9 8 7 6 5 4 3 2 1

Contents

Danger in the Garden............4

Poisonous—Don't Eat! 6

Deadly Wolfsbane 8

Poisonous Bulbs.................10

Deadly Berries...................12

Birds and Berries 14

Rosary Pea Seeds 16

A Very Dangerous Tree 18

Don't Touch! Don't Eat!.........20

Science Lab.....................22

Science Words 23

Index.............................24

Read More........................24

Learn More Online................24

About the Author.................24

Danger in the Garden

A farmer's goat has escaped from its pen.

It spots some pink flowers in a nearby garden and is about to take a bite.

Just then, the farmer appears and chases the goat away.

The animal doesn't know it, but it was very lucky.

The rhododendron flowers it was about to eat were **poisonous**!

Colorful rhododendron (*roh-duh-DEN-druhn*) plants grow in many gardens. These plants have flowers and leaves that are poisonous. If animals or humans eat them, they will vomit and get stomach pains. They might even die.

rhododendron flower

leaf

Why do you think a plant might have flowers or leaves that are poisonous?

Poisonous— Don't Eat!

Plants can't move away from animals that want to eat them.

So many plants get protection in other ways.

Some have flowers, leaves, stems, roots, or other parts that are poisonous.

If animals eat these plants and get sick, they usually learn not to eat them again.

Some plants, such as foxgloves, are very poisonous.

Every part of a foxglove contains poison.

flower

stem

leaf

roots

foxglove plant

Plants make seeds that grow into new plants. Being poisonous is one way some plants protect themselves from being eaten so that they can live long enough to make their seeds.

foxglove

Deadly Wolfsbane

One flowering plant that is very poisonous is aconitum (*ak*-uhn-EYE-tuhm).

This deadly plant is sometimes known as wolfsbane.

It got this name because people used part of the plant to kill wolves in ancient times.

Hunters dipped the tips of their arrows in the plant's poisonous juice.

wolf

a meadow
of aconitum

Every part
of an aconitum
plant is poisonous.
Eating just a tiny amount
can kill a person by
stopping the heart
from beating.

aconitum flowers

Poisonous Bulbs

Sometimes the most poisonous parts of a plant aren't the flowers or leaves.

Daffodils grow from a round **bulb** that is very poisonous.

The bulb looks a lot like an onion.

Both daffodil bulbs and onions grow underground.

Some unlucky people have dug up daffodil bulbs and eaten them, thinking they were onions!

daffodil

bulb

daffodils

daffodil bulb

onion

A person can get ill from eating just a small part of a daffodil bulb. The person will vomit and get bad stomach pains.

Deadly Berries

deadly nightshade berries

The seeds of some plants grow inside poisonous **berries**.

The berries protect the seeds from being eaten by people or animals.

One of the most dangerous berries in the world grows on the deadly nightshade plant.

This plant's berries look good enough to eat, and they taste sweet.

However, they are poisonous enough to kill a person.

People who eat deadly nightshade berries will vomit and become unable to speak. Their eyesight will get blurry, and they will feel very tired. Finally, they may fall into a deep sleep and die.

wild privet berries

bittersweet berries

lords and ladies berries

Do you think it's possible to tell if a berry is poisonous by how it looks? Which of the berries on this page do you think are poisonous?

(The answer is on page 24.)

Birds and Berries

Sometimes berries that are poisonous to most animals do not hurt birds.

For this reason, birds are able to help some plants spread their seeds to new places.

First, the birds swallow the berries whole without crunching up the seeds inside.

Then they fly to a new place, poop, and the seeds come out whole.

The seeds can now grow in the new place.

pokeweed berry

A person who eats pokeweed berries may vomit, get a headache and stomach pains—and even die. However, a bird can eat pokeweed berries without getting sick!

a mockingbird eating pokeweed berries

Rosary Pea Seeds

The seeds of the rosary pea plant contain one of the deadliest poisons in the world.

The seed's outer covering keeps the poison inside.

A person who swallows a seed whole might not be hurt by it.

When the seed's covering is broken, however, the poisonous insides of the seed are released.

Then swallowing just one seed would be enough to kill someone.

Rosary pea plants first grew in India and other countries in **Asia**. Now the plant is grown around the world. People in Asia use the seeds as beads to make jewelry.

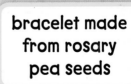

bracelet made from rosary pea seeds

rosary pea seeds

rosary pea seeds

Imagine you want to describe rosary pea seeds to a friend. What words would you use to tell how they look?

A Very Dangerous Tree

The poisonous manchineel (*man*-chuh-NEEL) tree can harm a person in many ways.

Eating the tree's fruit will make a person very sick—and may even cause death.

Like all trees, the manchineel's leaves and branches contain a liquid called **sap**.

When this tree's sap touches skin, however, it burns and makes the skin very sore.

Even raindrops that have fallen on the tree can mix with its poison and burn a person's skin.

Hundreds of years ago, warriors on Puerto Rico and other islands in the Caribbean Sea put the manchineel's poisonous sap on their arrows to kill their enemies.

NORTH AMERICA

Atlantic Ocean

Puerto Rico

Caribbean Sea

Pacific Ocean

SOUTH AMERICA

N
W · E
S

■ Where manchineel trees grow

manchineel tree

manchineel fruit

Manchineel trees sometimes have signs near them warning people that the trees are dangerous. Make a poster to warn people about manchineel trees. On your poster, draw a picture of the tree and write facts about why it is dangerous.

DANGER manchineel tree

Don't touch the tree. Its sap will burn your skin.

Don't eat the tree's fruit. It will make you sick.

fruit

Don't Touch! Don't Eat!

Poison ivy and poison oak are plants that grow in forests and fields.

People often touch these plants without knowing it.

Then, a few days later, a painful burning **rash** appears on their skin.

For many plants, being poisonous is the way they avoid being eaten.

Whether they have poisonous leaves, berries, or flowers, the message to animals is the same, "Stay away!"

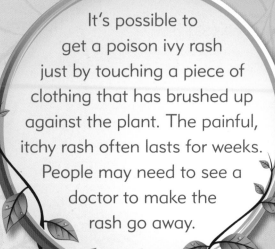

It's possible to get a poison ivy rash just by touching a piece of clothing that has brushed up against the plant. The painful, itchy rash often lasts for weeks. People may need to see a doctor to make the rash go away.

poison oak

poison ivy

poison ivy

Science Lab

A Poison Plant Book

Make your own book to tell friends and family members about poisonous plants.

Daffodil Bulb

A daffodil bulb looks like an onion.
Eating a small part of a daffodil bulb will make you vomit.

Include the plants you think are the most interesting from this book.

You can also use the Internet to find out about other poisonous plants.

How to Make Your Book

1. Have an adult staple two pieces of paper together.

2. Write the name of a poisonous plant at the top of each page.

3. Research facts about each plant.

4. Then write two or three sentences about each plant and draw a picture of it.

5. Share your book with friends and family members.

Think about these questions when you are researching poisonous plants. Include the answers in your information.

- Which part of the plant is poisonous?
- What happens to people or animals if they eat this plant?

Science Words

Asia (AY-zhuh) the world's largest continent (shown in red), which includes countries such as India and China

berries (BEHR-eez) small fruits, such as blueberries, blackberries, and grapes, that contain a seed or seeds

bulb (BUHLB) the rounded, underground part of some plants; food for the plant is stored in the bulb

poisonous (POI-zuhn-uhss) containing a substance that can harm or kill a living thing

rash (RASH) spots or red patches on skin that are usually itchy or sore

sap (SAP) a liquid that flows through a plant and carries water and nutrients—the substances plants need to live and grow

Index

aconitum 8–9
berries 12–13, 14–15, 20
birds 14–15
daffodil bulbs 10–11
deadly nightshade berries 12
death 4, 8–9, 12, 15, 16, 18
flowers 4–5, 6, 9, 10, 20

foxgloves 6–7
leaves 4–5, 6, 10, 18, 20
manchineel trees 18–19
onions 10–11
poison ivy 20–21
poison oak 20
pokeweed berries 14–15

rhododendrons 4
rosary pea seeds 16–17
sap 18
seeds 7, 12, 14, 16–17
stomach pains 4, 11, 15
vomiting 4, 11, 12, 15
wolfsbane 8

Read More

Day, Jeff. *Don't Touch That! The Book of Gross, Poisonous, and Downright Icky Plants and Critters.* Chicago: Chicago Review Press (2008).

Halfmann, Janet. *Plant Tricksters.* New York: Scholastic (2003).

Woolard, Sarah. *Dangerous Plants (DK ELT Graded Readers).* London: Dorling Kindersley (2000).

Learn More Online

To learn more about poisonous plants, visit
www.bearportpublishing.com/Plant-ology

Answers

Page 13: All of the berries are very poisonous! It's not possible to tell if a berry is poisonous by looking at it. That's why you should never taste a berry or any plant without knowing what kind it is and whether it is safe to eat.

About the Author

Ellen Lawrence lives in the United Kingdom. Her favorite books to write are those about nature and animals. In fact, the first book Ellen bought for herself, when she was six years old, was the story of a gorilla named Patty Cake that was born in New York's Central Park Zoo.

5732